BUILDING

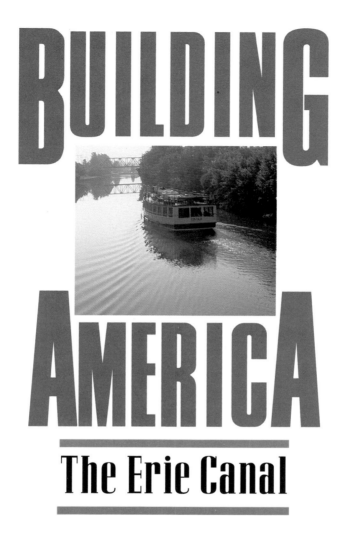

AMERICA

The Erie Canal

Craig A. Doherty and Katherine M. Doherty

A BLACKBIRCH PRESS BOOK

WOODBRIDGE, CONNECTICUT

To the memory of our friend, Donna Campbell

Special Thanks

The publisher would like to thank Laura Alvut, curator of collections and exhibitions, Erie Canal Museum, Syracuse, NY; Yvonne Murchison-Foote, Buffalo and Erie County Historical Society; Melody Kiepert, Erie Canal Village, Rome, NY; John L. Cardillo and Paul Sponable of the New York State Thruway Authority; and Donald A. Wilson, exhibit development services, The Exhibit Company, Syracuse, NY, for their valuable help and cooperation on this project.

Published by Blackbirch Press, Inc.
260 Amity Road
Woodbridge, CT 06525

© 1997 Blackbirch Press, Inc.
First Edition

Printed in the United States

10 9 8 7 6 5 4 3 2 1

Editorial Director: Bruce Glassman
Senior Editor: Nicole Bowen
Associate Editor: Elizabeth M. Taylor
Design and Production: Moore Graphics!

Photo Credits

Cover: New York State Thruway Authority; title page: New York State Department of Economic Development; contents page (from top to bottom): New York State Department of Economic Development; Erie Canal Museum, Syracuse, NY; Erie Canal Museum, Syracuse, NY; North Wind Picture Archives; North Wind Picture Archives; pages 4, 41 (bottom), 42–43: New York State Department of Economic Development; pages 7, 14, 21, 24: The Gayer Collection/NYS Canal Society; pages 8, 12, 13, 15, 22, 25, 26, 27, 30 (top), 32, 33, 34 (bottom), 35 (bottom), 38, 40, 41 (top): Erie Canal Museum, Syracuse, NY; pages 10, 17, 28, 30 (bottom), 31, 34 (top), 35 (top), 36: North Wind Picture Archives; page 19: Courtesy Erie Canal Village, Rome, NY; page 39: Courtesy of the Buffalo and Erie County Historical Society. Map by Blackbirch Graphics, Inc.

Library of Congress Cataloging-in-Publication Data
Doherty, Craig A.
   The Erie Canal / by Craig A. Doherty and Katherine M. Doherty. — 1st ed.
      p. cm.—(Building America)
   Includes bibliographical references and index.
   Summary: Discusses the history of this man-made waterway as well as basic engineering, architecture, and mechanical procedures involved in its construction.
   ISBN 1-56711-112-2 (alk. paper)
   1. Erie Canal (N.Y.)—History—Juvenile literature. [1. Erie Canal (N.Y.)—History.]
   I. Doherty, Katherine M. II. Title. III. Series: Doherty, Craig A. Building America.
TC625.E6A5 1997   95-25104
386'.48'09747—dc20   CIP
                                                   AC

Table of Contents

Introduction

In 1817, farmers of Western New York began the task of digging the Erie Canal. The canal would connect Lake Erie and the Atlantic Ocean, aiding in the expansion of the United States. In a time when transportation of goods and people was extremely difficult, the Erie Canal was a tremendous addition to the country's growth.

After the American Revolution, the United States had begun a westward expansion that would eventually lead it to the Pacific Ocean. In the early years of the republic, transportation to the west was a major problem. The Appalachian Mountains created a barrier from Maine all the way to Georgia. The few roads through the mountains were rough and difficult to travel. However, the reports of what lay

Opposite:
Boats still travel
through locks
on the Erie
Canal today.

to the west captured the imagination of people living to the east of the mountains. Talk of vast forests and the plains beyond appealed to people looking for new opportunities.

Breaks did occur in the mountains in the valley of the Hudson River and the valley of the Mohawk River in New York State. Early Dutch and English settlers had already moved up the Hudson using the river to transport themselves and the produce of their farms and factories. Other settlers had spread out along the Mohawk and other tributaries of the Hudson and settled much of Western New York State. What was needed was an easy way to connect the settlements of Western New York and beyond to the Atlantic Ocean.

In 1785, Christopher Colles, an engineer from Ireland, published an article calling for a canal along the Mohawk River valley from Albany to Oswego. (Canals are human-made waterways that allow boats to travel in areas where they couldn't before. They often parallel existing natural waterways that are not navigable.) The idea of a canal in New York State began to gain followers. One person credited with successfully promoting the idea at this early stage was Elkanah Watson. Early attempts to improve water travel included the formation of two companies to build short canals and locks. (A lock is an enclosure in a canal in which the water, along with the boats in the lock, can be raised or lowered to different water levels.) The companies chartered by the New York State legislature in 1792 were the Northern Inland Lock Navigation Company and the Western Inland Lock Navigation Company. The Northern company was to

work on connecting the Hudson River to Lake
Champlain, while the Western company was to connect the Hudson River with Lake Ontario.

The first undertaking of the Western company
was to build a set of locks so that boats could
bypass Little Falls on the Mohawk River. The company had to be bailed out financially by the state in
order to complete the job, but once finished, the
one-mile-long canal with five locks was a huge
success. Before the locks opened on the Mohawk,
goods had come down in small river boats, called
bateaux or Durham boats, poled by several people
and carrying about 3,000 pounds each. At Little Falls,
the contents of the boat had to be portaged, or carried, around the falls along with the boat. Once the
canal opened, barges carrying 10 to 11 tons could be
used, and the cost of shipping goods down the
Mohawk went from $14 a ton to $5 a ton.

*Before the Erie
Canal was built,
goods had to be
shipped down
the Mohawk by
small river boats.*

"Clinton's Folly"

The short canal around Little Falls showed many people in New York the advantages of an inland waterway. However, there were still many doubters who stood in the way of a longer canal. Jesse Hawley, a flour merchant in Geneva, New York, understood only too well the need for improved transportation between the inland farming areas and the urban markets of the coast. His business had gone bankrupt, in part, because of the high cost of shipping goods. Hawley ended up in debtors' prison for 20 months, and from his cell he wrote a series of articles calling for a canal connecting Lake Erie to the Hudson River. The 14 essays that he wrote using the penname "Hercules" were published in the *Genesee Messenger*, a local newspaper.

Opposite:
The canal around Little Falls on the Mohawk River showed people how useful a canal could be.

Top:
Governor De Witt Clinton
Bottom:
James Geddes

Finding the Route

Hawley described a route that was very close to the one that was later used for the Erie Canal. He also estimated the cost to build the canal at $6 million. Though the canal eventually cost more than $7 million to build, Hawley's estimate was impressive given that he was not an engineer.

Following Hawley's essays, in 1808, the New York State legislature passed a resolution to study the idea of a canal, and they appropriated $600 for a survey of two possible routes. Governor De Witt Clinton appointed Judge James Geddes to conduct the survey. Geddes had no formal training as an engineer, but, like many others of the time, he had acquired the skills necessary to survive in uncharted and unexplored lands. The first route that was considered would connect the Hudson River to Lake Ontario. The second was longer and more difficult; it connected the Hudson to Lake Erie.

The Lake Erie route was chosen over the Lake Ontario route despite the greater cost and difficulty of building the canal. This choice would benefit many more people in the western territories of Ohio, Michigan, and beyond. Connecting the Hudson with Lake Ontario would have primarily benefited the people of Canada. For the Lake Ontario route to reach those in the western territories, a canal would also have to be built around Niagara Falls to get from Lake Ontario to Lake Erie.

After Geddes's survey of possible routes, Governor Clinton and his supporters proposed that the state build a canal from Buffalo, on Lake Erie, to

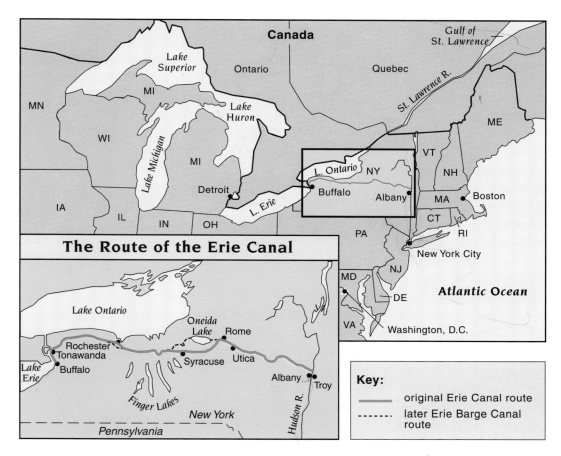

The Route of the Erie Canal

Key:
— original Erie Canal route
------- later Erie Barge Canal route

Albany, on the Hudson River. The canal would be 363 miles long, 40 feet wide at the top, 28 feet wide at the bottom, and 4 feet deep. The depth of 4 feet was decided on because it was as shallow as a canal could be and still be able to float boats. This was all that the planners felt they could afford.

The Erie Canal connected the Hudson River with the Great Lakes.

Finding the Money

Coming up with a plan for the Erie Canal proved easier than getting the money to build it. In 1809, a delegation from New York went to Washington, D.C., to see President Thomas Jefferson. Jefferson saw the benefit of the Erie Canal and felt it would help the young nation, however, he felt the federal government could not afford to finance such a large project.

Men work in a New York salt warehouse. A tax on the salt produced in Western New York raised money to build the canal.

Back in New York State, the canal supporters—led by Governor Clinton—realized that if they were to succeed, they would need to figure out a way to pay for the canal. Some wanted to form a private company to build it. Governor Clinton, however, felt that control of the building and operation of the canal should rest with the state. Clinton prevailed and came up with a series of taxes to fund construction. One of the important industries in Western New York, at the time, was the production of salt from underground salt springs. Clinton proposed a tax of 12½ cents per bushel on salt produced. The salt tax generated a lot of money, as did taxes on goods sold at auction, and a tax on steamship passengers.

With the money situation under control, it was time to start digging the canal. The War of 1812 intervened, however, and during the war years (1812–1815), work was put on hold. As soon as the war ended, it was time to get out the shovels and go to work. The conflict had brought home the point that it was extremely important to have a better transportation system in the United States. During the war, it had been very difficult to move people and supplies inland.

Getting Ready

The New York State legislature passed the Canal Bill of 1817, and the commission that had been set up to oversee the construction of the canal in 1810 was finally ready to begin work. During the next eight years, workers built 363 miles of canal that included 83 locks. The locks were needed to raise and lower the canal boats up and down over the varied topography of Upstate New York. Lake Erie is 565 feet higher than the Hudson River at Albany. Each lock could raise or lower a boat 6 to 12 feet, depending on the difference in height of the next section of the canal. If the difference was greater than one lock could handle, then a series of locks were built together.

In addition to digging the canal and building the locks, 18 aqueducts had to be constructed. An aqueduct is a raised structure designed to carry water. The 18 aqueducts of the Erie Canal were built big enough to allow the canal boats to float over places where digging and locks would not work—low valleys, rough ground, and usually over other bodies of water.

Some aqueducts carried canal boats over other waterways.

HOW LOCKS WORK

There were 83 locks on the original Erie Canal; without them a canal across New York would have been impossible. Locks allow the canal boats to move from a section of the canal that is at one level to a section that is either higher or lower. The locks on the Erie Canal were built to raise or lower a boat between 6 and 12 feet. If the difference in the two sections of the canal was greater than 12 feet, two or more locks would be built together.

A lock is a watertight section of a canal with gates at either end. The water level in it is changed to raise and lower the boats traveling the canal. On the Erie Canal, the locks were built to raise or lower just one boat at a time.

To operate the lock, the lock tenders would open the lower gate and a boat would enter. When the boat was inside, the gates would be shut. Then a sluice (a small gate in the door) would be opened, allowing water from the higher section of the canal to enter the lock. As the lock filled, the boat would come up with the level of the water. When the water inside was the same height as the water of the upper level of the canal, the upper gate would be opened.

The boat in the lock would continue on its way, and a boat from the upper level would enter the lock. The upper sluice would be closed, and a lower sluice would be opened. The water would run out of the lock until the water inside matched the level of the water in the lower section of the canal. When the levels matched, the lower gate was opened and the boat would go on its way. In the busiest times of the year, as many as 250 boats a day would pass through a lock, which meant the level of the water would be raised and lowered 125 times!

Locks were needed along the Erie Canal to raise and lower boats.

Experts in Europe, where many canals had already been built, were doubtful of the Erie Canal's success. Those who thought New York's canal builders, most of whom were amateurs, had a chance of succeeding felt it would take them at least 20 years. In fact, it only took eight years. This achievement was a testament to the ingenuity and resourcefulness of those who built what was then the longest modern canal in the world.

In the summer of 1817, when work began on the project, there were no bulldozers or other power equipment. People working with shovels, picks, axes, and horses had to clear a 60-foot-wide track—much of it through previously untouched wilderness. At the time the canal was begun, there wasn't even a stagecoach line between Buffalo and Albany. The Canal Commission decided to start in the middle of the canal route where there was a relatively flat stretch that was 94 miles long. Rome, New York, is situated in this section and was the starting point for the digging. The official groundbreaking ceremony was held there on July 4, 1817.

The official groundbreaking for the Erie Canal was held July 4, 1817, in Rome, New York.

Digging the Ditch

The members of the commission believed that starting in the middle would accomplish two objectives. First, the local people could use the canal almost immediately, even if it didn't connect to other waterways. Also, the flat terrain of this area would allow for the greatest results in the shortest time.

The commission realized that the farmers in the area had little in the way of off-farm work available, so they allowed individuals to bid on the digging of a quarter of a mile at a time. More than 50 people were awarded contracts to work on the first 58 miles. The commission advanced funds to successful bidders so that they could buy horses, mules, and tools and employ laborers. Most of them later rebid on other sections. In this way, the canal brought a higher level of prosperity to the farmers while they worked on the project, which, in turn, created important political support.

Working alongside the farmers was a team of engineers. Most of the engineers who worked on the construction of the canal had little or no formal training in civil engineering (the branch of engineering that deals with the building of roads, bridges, dams, canals, and other large public works). It has been said that the building of the Erie Canal was the first "school of civil engineering" in the United States. Benjamin Wright was the chief engineer for the middle section, and he brought the most experience to the job. After making the initial survey (land study) in 1808, James Geddes stayed with the project and designed many of the mechanical structures on the canal. Nathan S. Roberts, another engineer, was responsible for designing one of the canal's most amazing features: a series of five double locks that would raise and lower the canal boats over the 76-foot-high rock ridge at Lockport.

The engineers staked out the 60-foot-wide path. It was important to keep the canal as straight as possible, and critically important to keep everything level. Someone had suggested that the waterway should be designed with a continuous incline, downhill from Buffalo to Albany. Although this idea might have been appealing, it was not practical—especially for those who would want to ship goods up the incline. A level canal would make it much easier to maintain the water supply and keep the boats floating. The faster-moving water would have caused erosion, quickly eating away the earthen sides of the canal.

Five double locks had to be built through the rock ridge at Lockport.

Trees were cut, stumps were pulled, hills were leveled, and holes were filled in before the workers could begin to dig the ditch and make the embankments. In addition to the 40-foot-wide canal, the workers also had to build a 10-foot-wide towpath along one side of the canal and clear an additional 10-foot work area. Although the goods would move by boat, the boats would be pulled by horses and mules. The canal boats did not have engines, sails, or oars.

Innovative Solutions

During the first season, 15 miles of canal were completed, and many valuable lessons were learned. In part, because they were farmers, and in part because they needed a way to be more efficient if they were to make a profit on their contracts, the workers began using their horses, plows, and scrapers to dig. First, the workers would plow up the stretch of canal that they were working on, then they would hitch a scraper to their team and pull the loosened dirt up the sides of the embankment. Once the loose soil was removed, they would hitch up the plows again and loosen more. This proved much faster than hand shovels and wheelbarrows, and the fact that the horses and oxen used to pull the plows and scrapers packed down the soil on the embankments provided an unexpected benefit. One canal worker even devised a modified plow that had cutting blades attached to it that would cut through the roots of the brush along the route.

The trees and tree stumps were a bigger problem that also called for an ingenious solution. Much of the canal route passed through forests of old, large hardwoods. Cutting these trees down with axes was too time consuming so two devices were created for the job. One pulled down the trees, while the other pulled out the stumps. To pull down the trees, a cable was attached to the top of the tree. Then the cable was attached to a roller, and a mechanical device called an endless screw was used to turn the roller and pull the cable. The pressure created by the device pulled down the trees.

The stump puller was equally inventive. It was a device mounted on 16-foot-high wheels, and between the wheels was a 30-foot-long, 20-inch-thick axle. In the center of the axle was a 14-foot-diameter spool. A team of horses or oxen were attached to a cable that

wound around the spool. As they turned the spool, the cable that ran from the axle to the stump was wound in. One person who worked on the canal recalled that his work gang of 7 laborers and 4 horses could pull 40 tree stumps a day.

The stump puller was just one of several inventions that were created to help build the canal.

A New Labor Force

After the first season, everyone involved with the project felt good. They had learned a lot about canal building, and they realized that they would be able to get the job done. There were, however, still problems that had to be solved.

One of the major problems for the engineers was working with the more than 50 independent contractors. Most of these people were farmers who put their farms ahead of the canal. If there was work that needed to be done at home, they would take time off from the canal to do it. A high turnover in the labor force meant that valuable time was always being wasted showing new workers what to do. The engineers wanted a full-time work force that would be more stable and reliable than the farmers were.

The solution was found in the cities. Many people living in the cities had recently arrived in the United States and needed jobs. New York, Boston, and Philadelphia all had large populations of immigrants, many of whom were living in slumlike conditions. These people were recruited to work on construction. Governor Clinton even went as far as releasing people from prison if their offense was not too serious and if they were willing to work off the rest of their sentence on the Erie Canal. Hundreds of prisoners took the governor up on his offer, and they were paid the same wages as the other workers were.

There were two systems of pay for the workers. A laborer could work for a wage of 37½ cents to 50 cents a day, or he could choose to be paid by the amount of material he removed from the canal. One team of 3 workers who chose to be paid by volume dug out 3 rods (a rod is a surveying measurement of 16½ feet) of the canal in 5½ days. They moved 250 cubic yards of material and were paid 12½ cents per yard. That came out to $1.89 per day, per worker.

Death in the Swamps

Many workers during the 1818 and 1819 digging seasons were not as productive. West of Syracuse, Montezuma Swamp presented a new set of difficulties for the canal builders. The oozing mud of the swamp was difficult to remove, and workers often found themselves trying to dig while standing chest-deep in water. Much worse than the water and mud were the diseases that struck as many as 1,000 workers during the summer of 1819. Malaria, typhoid fever, pneumonia, and other diseases killed many. The exact number who

died is not known, and most of the dead were buried in unmarked graves along the canal. Mosquitoes were a large part of the problem, as some of them transmitted malaria with their bites.

Conditions were so bad digging the canal through Montezuma Swamp that it became very difficult to get replacement workers for those who had died or were too sick to work. Some critics referred to the canal as "Clinton's Folly" and to the various diseases encountered in the swamp as "De Witt's diseases."

The coming of colder weather in the fall of 1819 was the biggest help to the problems of the swamp. The first frost finished off the mosquitoes for the year. The frost also hardened the ground and made it easier to remove—much easier than the oozing mud the workers had been fighting since they entered the wet and difficult area.

This photo shows construction of the Erie Barge Canal in Montezuma Swamp. It was still a tough place to work, but not as bad as when the Erie Canal had first been built through the swamp almost 100 years earlier.

The Canal Opens

Despite the hardships, the engineers and the construction crews overcame the obstacles of the swamp. On April 21, 1820, the first passenger boat, the *Chief Engineer of Rome*, traveled from Rome west to Syracuse. On July 4, 1820, Governor Clinton came to Rome for the official grand opening of that section of the canal and participated in a 73-boat procession.

Once a section of the canal was operational—and tolls were collected from the boats using the waterway—many of the critics were quieted, and work on the rest of the project continued. One of the most interesting features of the Erie Canal was the system of 18 aqueducts that carried the canal above ground level. One of the longest was the 802-foot-long aqueduct over the Genesee River at Rochester. It used nine arches, each with a span of 50 feet.

Opposite:
In 1823, when the aqueduct over the Genesee River at Rochester was finished, it was one of the longest on the Erie Canal.

23

The massive stones used to build the aqueduct had to be quarried and shaped by hand. Auburn State Prison provided 150 convicts to do the stone work. Many people in Rochester were outraged that these criminals were working in their community. Despite the criticism of the convict labor, the people of Rochester were excited about the canal reaching their town. Within a year, more than 100 new houses had been built and the economy of the area was booming. The positive economic impact of the canal was felt all along its path.

The Chief Engineer of Rome *was built specifically to carry passengers on the canal. It was 76 feet long and 14 feet wide.*

Stone and Mortar

For most of the route, the canal was simply a ditch with banks made from the soil along the way. In some stretches where the engineers were worried about the soil holding water, mud with a higher clay content was added to the banks. The two areas of the canal where dirt banks would not work were the aqueducts and the locks. They had to be made of stone and mortar.

High-grade limestone was quarried near Medina, New York, and it was used throughout the canal for locks, aqueducts, and water-control devices. Cement created another problem for the engineers to solve. Canvass White, who was an assistant engineer, had been sent to Europe to examine the canal-building techniques used there. He returned with a lot of helpful information. Probably White's biggest contribution to the building of the canal was his development of a local source for hydraulic cement. Hydraulic cement is cement that will harden under water. Before this discovery, there had been no American source of hydraulic cement, and bringing it from Europe would have cost too much. A type of rock known as "meagre limestone" was found suitable for making hydraulic cement, and White developed a formula for using it. Almost half a million bushels of White's cement were used in building the Erie Canal. It was far superior to the lime mortar that had previously been used, and maybe even better than that used by the European builders.

Limestone quarried in Medina, New York, was used to build aqueducts and locks.

The Skyway

By 1820, the easy sections of the canal were finished and in use, but the engineers still faced challenges along the western end of the canal. One of the problem areas was the Irondequoit Valley near Rochester. The valley was 4,950 feet wide. At first, the plan was to build an aqueduct over the valley and then bring in enough dirt to bury it, helping to support and protect it from the wind. However, the engineers decided that this was impractical and were forced to come up with an alternative.

The solution they finally devised called for a solid earthen and stone embankment. The only break in the embankment would be a stone culvert that allowed Irondequoit Creek to continue to flow down the valley. The stone culvert was 245 feet long, the width of the embankment at its base. At the top of the embankment, 76 feet above the valley, it narrowed so there was just room for the canal and the towpath. Suitable soil to build this "skyway," as it came to be called, was hauled in from miles around.

Blasting Through

In places such as the Irondequoit Valley, material had to be hauled in to build the canal; in other places, like Lockport, huge quantities of stone had to be removed. The workers used a number of techniques for removing solid rock. In some places, they used hammers and stone chisels. In other places, gunpowder was used to blast apart the rock. The workers were also able to use the forces of nature to their advantage. In the winter, they drilled

A huge amount of stone had to be removed to build the canal west of Lockport.

THE BIRTH OF LOCKPORT

One of the largest obstacles faced by the builders of the Erie Canal was getting boats up and down the big ridge of rock located about 17 miles east of Niagara Falls. This is known as the Niagara Escarpment and is in part responsible for Niagara Falls. At the point where the canal meets the escarpment, the solid rock rises almost 70 feet. Nathan Roberts, one of the engineers working on the canal, designed a series of five double locks to raise and lower the boats.

When Roberts and the first workers arrived at the future site of the

Entrance to the harbor, Lockport

locks in July 1821, there were three families living in the area. By January 1822, there were more than 300 families living there, and that did not include the temporary laborers who were working on the locks. This new town took its name from the locks that made it famous, becoming Lockport, New York.

As the workers drilled and blasted through the solid rock, the town prospered. After the canal opened, Lockport continued to grow, and the completed locks became one of the most amazing accomplishments of the Erie Canal.

holes in the rock, poured in water, and hoped that the force of the expanding ice would split it.

Gunpowder was not that effective at blasting apart solid stone. Luckily, at Lockport, the engineers were able to get a new blasting powder that had recently been developed by the Du Pont Company. The rock at Lockport was so hard that it is doubtful if they would have been able to remove it without the blasting powder. Unfortunately, at the time the canal was built, not many people were experienced with using gun powder and blasting powder, and many accidents resulted.

From Lake Erie to the Hudson River

In fall of 1825, the canal was completed, and a ten-day celebration was held just before the canal was closed down for the winter. The celebration was led by the *Seneca Chief*, which started in Buffalo on October 26, 1825. Governor Clinton, Jesse Hawley, and other dignitaries were on board. The *Seneca Chief* was accompanied by a flotilla of other boats that grew as it traveled eastward along the Erie Canal. Each community along the way held celebrations.

The beginning of the celebration in Buffalo was announced in New York City in a unique way. The

Opposite:
The celebration of the opening of the canal began on October 26, 1825.

29

Top:
The "Wedding of the Waters" was part of the canal's opening ceremonies.

Bottom:
City Hall in New York City was lit up for the Erie Canal celebration of 1825.

telegraph had not yet been invented, so cannons were spaced out along the canal and the Hudson River. When the *Seneca Chief* began its historic voyage, the first cannon was fired. When the people at the second cannon heard the shot fired by the first cannon, they fired, and so on down the canal and river. It took 1 hour and 20 minutes for the series of cannon shots to reach New York City and complete the announcement.

One of the largest celebrations was held in Albany, where tables were set for 600 people on the Columbia Street Bridge over the Hudson. When the *Seneca Chief* arrived in New York City on November 4, 1825, a number of festivities were held, including concerts, balls, fireworks, and most symbolically a ceremony called the "Wedding of the Waters." Governor Clinton had brought a container of Lake

Canal boats were loaded up with grain from lake ships in Buffalo.

Erie water with him and had vials of water from rivers around the world. The *Seneca Chief* was towed out to where the Hudson joins the Atlantic, and members of the Canal Commission poured the containers into the ocean. This symbolically joined Lake Erie with the Atlantic Ocean and the other great waterways of the world.

Beyond Expectations

The canal was a huge success even before it was completed in 1825. It cost the state of New York more than $7 million to build, but in 1824, they were able to collect $300,000 in tolls. In 1826—the first full year of operation—the state collected more than $1 million. By 1836, the debts of the project had been paid off, and the surplus revenues were helping to cover other state expenses.

The tolls for freight on the canal were determined by weight. Special weighlocks were built at Albany, West Troy, Rochester, Syracuse, and Utica. Every spring, the boats on the canal would be weighed empty. To

"Low Bridge, Ev'rybody Down"

Canal bridges were so low that people sailing under them had to duck.

Even before the canal was finished, people began singing songs about it. Most of the songs were set to tunes that were well known to the people of the time. One early song that was supposedly sung by workers as they dug through deadly Montezuma Swamp started with the following verse:

> We are digging the Ditch through the mire;
> Through the mud and the slime and the
>   mire, by heck!
> And the mud is our principal hire;
> Up our pants, in our shirts, down our neck,
>   by heck!

> We are digging the Ditch through the
>   gravel,
> So the people and freight can travel.

As people traveled along the canal they constantly had to be reminded to duck their heads as they passed under the many low bridges. Today, the chorus of the best-known song about the Erie Canal deals with the low bridges. It begins:

> Low bridge, ev'rybody down,
> Low bridge, we must be getting near a
>   town,
> You can always tell your neighbor,
> You can always tell your pal,
> If he's ever navigated on the Erie Canal.

(One could always tell who had ridden the canal before because if someone said "low bridge," they would duck.) In addition to the songs that were sung about the Erie Canal, many famous writers also gave it their attention. Mark Twain wrote a poem, "The Aged Pilot Man," about an Erie Canal boatman, and Herman Melville mentioned the canal in his classic book *Moby Dick*.

do this, a boat would enter the weighlock and then the water would be drained out, leaving the boat sitting on a scale. There, its weight would be recorded. When the barges came along the canal loaded, they would again be weighed, and the toll would be computed on the difference between the boat's loaded and empty weight.

The average canal cargo boat might carry 100,000 pounds of freight. In 1836, the toll on flour and wheat

In 1844, the first novel written entirely about the Erie Canal was published. *Marco Paul's Travels and Adventures in the Pursuit of Knowledge on the Erie Canal* was about a boy named Marco Paul who travels along the Erie Canal with his guardian and has a variety of adventures.

Many of the songs and at least one play dealt with the wilder side of life on the canal, especially on some of the packet boats (passenger boats). Put on in 1828, the play was a farce (an exaggerated comedy) called *A Trip to Niagara*.

Some of the people working the boats on the canal had been ocean-traveling sailors before settling in to work on the calm and shallow waters of the Erie Canal. Some of these men adapted the songs and chanteys of the high seas to the canal. For sailors who had faced the true dangers of the wide oceans, the four-foot-deep canal was pretty tame. The song "The Raging Canal," written and sung by P. Morris, makes fun of the canal's calm waters.

The many songs, stories, plays, and books about the Erie Canal remind us that during its heyday it was an extremely important part of people's lives. For the men, women, and children who worked their boats up and down the waterway, it was their front yard and their livelihood.

Canal boats usually had two mules so the animals could be alternated.

was 4.5 mills per 1,000 pounds per mile (a mill is one tenth of a cent). The toll for other freight was double the rate for flour and wheat. The toll for a boat carrying 100,000 pounds of flour or wheat for the entire 363 miles of the canal would have been $163.35. Passenger traffic was also important on the canal. Passenger boats, called packets, paid a toll of 15 cents per mile east of Utica and 8 cents per mile west

FROM THE LAKES TO THE HUDSON.—A GRAIN-BOAT ON THE ERIE CANAL.—SKETCHED BY JOSEPH BECKER.

Top:
Grain was carried east on the canal.
Bottom:
A canal packet loaded with tourists cruises the waterway.

of Utica. In addition, packets paid an additional two mills per passenger, per mile.

In 1826, there were 160 freight boats using the Erie Canal and a small number of packets. The packet boats were lighter and traveled faster. They were also given preferential treatment at the locks. Many of the boats that traveled the canal were the same size, which was determined by the dimensions of the canal and its locks. The maximum size was 14 feet wide and 80 feet long. The boats were also limited by the 4-foot depth of the canal and by the height of the bridges. In attempting to save money, the Canal Commission required bridges to be only 7 feet above the water.

By 1836, there were more than 3,000 boats traveling back and forth on the canal. Even with that many boats, the canal couldn't meet the demand for transportation. The barges traveling east carried the produce of the farms and forests surrounding the Great Lakes. In 1840, flour and wheat made up approximately one third of the eastbound cargo, while salt and manufactured goods made up the bulk of what was shipped west. Traffic was so heavy that it was not unusual for a lock to have 250 boats a day pass through.

Hurry-up—Maintaining the Canal

Maintenance kept many workers busy throughout the year. During the nine-month season that the canal was open, breaks in the banks of the canal were frequent. Special boats, called "hurry-up boats," would rush to any problems and repair them. In addition to repairs, the canal needed constant attention. Silt, sandbars, and weeds that grew in the water all created problems that maintenance crews had to solve.

Upgrading the Canal

Prosperity grew all along the canal. Boatyards built barges as fast as they could, and other industries moved to the area to take advantage of the quick and efficient transportation provided by the waterway. When the canal was completed, construction began on a series of feeder canals. The Oswego Canal, opened in 1828, was 24 miles long and connected the Erie Canal with Lake Ontario. The Cayuga and Seneca Canal joined the largest of the Finger Lakes to the canal, and it also opened in 1828. In

Opposite:
The canal brought prosperity to cities and towns all along its route. This picture shows Buffalo in the 1880s.

37

LIFE ON THE ERIE CANAL

At one time, more than 50,000 people depended on the Erie Canal for their income. A whole new culture evolved around canal life. For many, their boats were their homes, and the entire family was involved. Typically, the father would be the captain and steersman, while the mother cooked for the crew and her family. The cabin of the boat had a stove for cooking, a table for eating, and bunks for sleeping. Most of the freight boats had another cabin for a spare pair of mules. One pair would pull the boat, while the other team ate and rested.

Children too young to work would wear a harness attached to the boat by a rope—that way if they fell off, it would be easy to pull them out of the water. As soon as they were eight-to-ten years old, children would begin to work in the family business. The first job for many children was that of "hoggee." A hoggee was the person who walked the towpath alongside the team of mules or horses and made sure that they kept going at a steady pace.

A report in 1848 estimated that there were 10,000 boys employed on the Erie Canal. Some of these young workers died in the course of a season: The days were very hard; disease, too little food, and too much work were often problems on boats that hired help. The going rate for hoggees was only seven-to-ten dollars a month.

Serious problems arose during the winter when the canal would have to shut down because the water froze. The out-of-work children were turned loose in the towns along the canal. Concerned citizens suggested building dorms for the boys.

For those who traveled on the passenger boats, or packets, the canal was an exciting place. There

Whole families lived and worked on the canal boats.

1833, the Chemung Canal gave the people of the Elmira, New York, area a link to the Erie Canal. A five-mile-long canal connected Oneida Lake to the canal in 1835. In 1837, the Chenango Canal joined the Susquehana River to the Erie Canal at Utica. The Genesee Canal was started in 1837 and ran from Rochester to the Alleghany River. By 1836, traffic had

Mule teams pulled the canal boats.

were often gambling and entertainment on the packets.

In addition to the people who worked on the boats, it took many people to operate the Erie Canal. Engineers were employed to deal with problems that came up, and there needed to be lock tenders at every lock and weigh station. There also had to be maintenance crews ready to deal with the problems of an earthen-walled canal.

To keep tabs on the canal, "towpath walkers" were employed. They searched for leaks in the sides of the canal. When they spotted a

leak or some other sort of problem, they would send for one of the many "hurry-up boats" stationed along the canal. The hurry-up boats would do just that; they would hurry-up to the location of the leak and fix it.

All along the canal, businesses opened up to cater to the traffic. The people on the boats needed food and other supplies. Boat building also became an important industry. Businesses along the route prospered because they could easily and cheaply ship their goods west to the frontier or east through New York City to the rest of the world.

grown so much along the canal that the New York State legislature voted to enlarge it. It was widened to 70 feet, and the depth was increased to 7 feet.

Traffic on the canal continued to increase despite competition from the growing network of railroads. By the end of the Civil War in 1865, there were 7,000 boats working the Erie Canal. It was said that if you

stood on any of the bridges over the canal during the busiest season, you would see a solid line of boats stretching as far as you could see in both directions.

In the 1890s, the Erie Canal was enlarged again, but it still could not meet the demand for shipping. In 1918, New York State replaced the Erie Canal with a new, modern canal that could accommodate much larger vessels and handle self-propelled boats. That year, the Erie Barge Canal opened. In some places, it ran along the existing route; in other areas, a new route had been laid out. The Barge Canal was an important link to the Great Lakes until 1959. In that year, the last section of the St. Lawrence Seaway was completed, and ocean-going ships could travel directly from the Atlantic Ocean

Top:
During the busy season, the canal would be filled with a solid line of boats.
Bottom:
Steam and diesel power replaced mules on the Barge Canal.

up the St. Lawrence River and into the Great Lakes.

Today, the Barge Canal is used almost exclusively for recreational boating. Visitors can still watch the locks fill and empty as boats travel through Lockport—where a small canal museum is now located. There is also a canal museum in Syracuse housed in the only surviving old weighlock building. The sections of the Erie Canal that still exist have become favorite places for canoers and those who use the old towpath for a hiking trail. In 1967, Old Erie Canal State Park was created on a 35-mile stretch of the canal, running from just outside Syracuse to Rome. It commemorates what had at one time been called "Clinton's Folly" but went on to become one of the most important links in the building of America.

Top: *The impressive series of five locks at Lockport was replaced by two locks.* **Bottom:** *Lock tenders still work along the canal today.*

Today, most boats travel the canal for sightseeing or recreational purposes.

GLOSSARY

aqueduct A raised structure designed to carry water.

arch A rounded space between two supporting columns used to distribute the weight of the structure.

blasting powder An explosive form of gunpowder.

canal A human-made waterway.

chantey A sailor's song.

debtor's prison Special prisons that were set up for people who could not pay their debts.

endless screw A mechanical device that uses screw threads to continually turn a set of gears.

engineer (civil) A person who deals with the design and construction of large public works such as highways, bridges, and canals.

escarpment A steep slope or cliff.

freight boat A vessel designed to carry goods rather than people.

hoggees People who walked the towpaths guiding the animal teams that pulled the boats.

hurry-up boats Special boats that were sent quickly to fix any problems with the canal.

hydraulic cement A specially formulated cement that dries hard underwater.

immigrant A person who leaves his or her native land and comes to another country.

limestone A rock that is used in the manufacture of cement.

lock A structure for lifting and lowering boats between varying levels of a canal.

mill A measurement of money equal to one tenth of a cent.

navigate To control the course of a boat, ship, or other vessel.

packet boat A canal boat designed for carrying passengers.

portage The act of carrying a boat and its contents around an unnavigable stretch of water or from one body of water to another.

stump puller A large device created by the canal builders to pull out the stumps of trees.

towpath walkers Workers who walked the banks of a canal keeping an eye out for any problems that might need attention.

towpath The widened area on the bank of a canal where the animal teams pulling the boats walked.

tributary A smaller river or stream that empties into a larger one.

weighlock A special lock that contained scales for weighing freight boats.

CHRONOLOGY

1785 Christopher Colles publishes report suggesting a canal in the Mohawk River valley.

1792 New York State legislature creates two canal companies.

1793–1796 The Western Inland Lock Navigation Co. builds locks around Little Falls.

1806–1807 Jesse Hawley suggests a canal be built from Lake Erie to the Hudson River.

1808 New York State legislature appropriates $600 to survey possible canal routes.

James Geddes is appointed to survey possible canal routes.

1809 Delegation is sent to Washington, D.C., to ask the president for federal help in building the canal.

1810 A commission is formed to oversee the building of the canal.

1812–1815 War of 1812 delays the beginning of construction.

1816 New bill is introduced to start work on the canal.

1817 April 15 Canal Bill of 1817 passes and work on the canal can finally begin.

July 4 Official groundbreaking ceremony at Rome, New York; construction starts on the middle section of the canal.

1819 October 23 Canal opens between Utica and Rome.

1820 April 21 First passenger boat goes from Rome to Syracuse on the Erie Canal.

1822 Construction of the western end of the canal begins.

October Irondequoit Creek skyway is completed.

1823 August Work begins to connect Buffalo to the Erie Canal.

October Canal opens from Rochester west to Brockport.

1824 September Canal opens from Brockport to Lockport.

1825 June Work at Lockport is completed.

October 26–November 4 Celebration of the completion of the Erie Canal.

1835–1862 Erie Canal enlarged.

1902–1917 Erie Canal expanded.

1917 Erie Canal closed.

1918 Erie Barge Canal is complete and replaces old Erie Canal.

1959 St. Lawrence Seaway is completed, making barge canal obsolete as as a shipping route.

1967 Old Erie Canal State Park is created.

FURTHER READING

Avakian, Monique, and Carter Smith, III. *A Historical Album of New York*.
  Brookfield, CT: Millbrook Press, 1993.

Cooper, J. *Canals*. Vero Beach, FL: Rourke, 1991.

Nirgiotis, Nicholas. *Erie Canal: Gateway to the West*. New York:
  Franklin Watts, 1993.

Spangenburg, Ray, and Diane K. Moser. *The Story of America's Canals*.
  New York: Facts On File, 1992.

Spier, Peter. *The Erie Canal*. New York: Doubleday, 1990.

Stein, R. Conrad. *The Story of the Erie Canal*. Chicago:
  Childrens Press, 1985.

SOURCE NOTES

Albino, Joseph. "The Old Erie Canal State Park." *Conservationist* July/August 1989, p. 25.

Clark, Laura L. "Delineation of the Proposed Ohio and Erie Canal." *Papers and Proceedings of the
  Applied Geography Conference*. 1993, vol. 16, p. 32.

Ehman, James. *Chattey's Island*. New York: Ticknor & Fields, 1982.

Erie Canal Museum: Photos from the Collection. Syracuse, NY: Erie Canal Museum, 1989.

Gordon, John Steele. "Real Estate: Where and When." *American Heritage*. November 1992, 18–22.

Heiman, Michael K. "Erie Canal." *WorldBook Information Finder* [CD-ROM], 1993.

Miller, Nathan. *The Enterprise of a Free People: Aspects of Economic Development in New York State
  during the Canal Period, 1792–1838*. Ithaca, NY: Cornell University Press, 1962.

Nirgiotis, Nicholas. *Erie Canal: Gateway to the West*. New York: Franklin Watts, 1993.

Prindle, Tom. "Reopening the Doors of History." *Sea History*. Winter 1994, n. 72, p. 16.

Shaw, Ronald E. *Erie Water West: A History of the Erie Canal 1792–1854*. Lexington:
  University Press of Kentucky, 1990.

Trotta, Paul D. "Canal." *WorldBook Information Finder* [CD-ROM], 1993.

Verhovek, Sam Howe. "On Erie Canal, Where Mules Once Toiled." *New York Times*, August 19, 1989.

———. "Plan to Revive Erie Canal: Add Tollbooths to Lock?." *New York Times*,
  October 31, 1991.

Way, Peter. "Evil Humors and Ardent Spirits." *Journal of American History*, March 1993, vol. 79,
  n. 4, p. 1397.

Wyld, Lionel D. *Low Bridge: Folklore and the Erie Canal*. Syracuse University Press, 1962.

INDEX